Om Shri Ganeshaya Namah

Wisdom Nuggets of Swami Tapovan-ji Maharaj - and Śrīmad Bhagavad Gita

Compiled & Annotated by Pt. Aswadhnath Anantajit

Anjaneya Prakash Publications

Print Edition, January 2024

Published by Anjaneyar Prakash Publications

Images courtesy public domain

EPIGRAPH

Aum Asato ma sad-gamaya;
Tamaso ma jyotir-gamaya;
Mrityor-ma amrutam gamaya
Aum
Shanti, Shanti, Shanti

Aum
Lead me from unreal to real;
Lead me from darkness to light;
Lead me from death to immortality
Aum
Peace, Peace, Peace

CONTENTS

ACKNOWLEDGEMENTS

I acknowledge the Grace of my Guru due to which I gained little knowledge, insights and wisdom that I can share with others.

I acknowledge my lineage deity, my ancestors especially my grandfather Pashupati Nath and my grandmother Pushpa and ancestors of the land I live and work in.

I acknowledge my wife who really is my better half and has stood by me through thick and thin that life has given us.

I acknowledge the editors of Anjaneya Prakash Publications for their wonderful work towards publishing this book.

1. INTRODUCTION

The current compilation of wisdom words are from Swami Tapovan-ji Maharaj, who to me is a Paramhamsa, an enlightened being. As there is an old saying that you can learn about a tree from it's fruits, one of His famous disciples is Swami Chinmayananda Maharaj, who founded the world-wide organisation, Chinmaya Mission, spreading spirituality and Hindu philosophy of life.

Swami Tapovan-ji Maharaj was born in 1889 in Kerala, one of the southern states of India. He showed high inclination towards spirituality from early childhood. He did home schooling and learnt English, Malayalam (the native language of Kerala) and Sanskrit. He also learned poetry, drama, grammar and logic but spent most of His time in doing spiritual practices.

After both His parents passed away and his younger brother got settled in life, Swami Tapovan-ji Maharaj left Kerala on the day of Janmasthami, the birthday of Lord Shri Krishna that usually falls in the months of August-September (months vary as per the Hindu lunar calendar) in 1923 to become a renunciate.

He loved the Himalayas and remained there for the rest of His life. He documented some of His

Himalayan travels to help spiritual aspirants understand not just the beauty of Himalayas but also It's sacredness and the various pilgrim spots and areas. These were document in books called '*Wanderings in the Himalayas*' and '*Kailasa Yatra*'.

Swami Tapovan-ji Maharaj left His mortal body in the early hours of 16 January 1957, which was a full moon day.

This compilation is a small dedication to Swami Tapovan-ji Maharaj on His 100th year of leaving home to become a renunciate in the months of August-September (Janmasthami day) in 1923. Personally, I have a passion for teachings of Śrīmad Bhagavad Gita and hence have included some verses from it that are in alignment with wisdom words of Swami Tapovan-ji Maharaj.

The wisdom nuggets and brief annotations in the current compilation is how I see and understand from my perspective only. Each one of us may understand and interpret differently based on their own personal experiences in current and past lifetime. Hence, if someone interprets the wisdom nuggets of Swami Tapovan-ji Maharaj differently than what I have, is perfectly understandable.

2 GOD / BRAHMAN

Swami Tapovan-ji Maharaj saw God or Brahman everywhere especially in nature. According to Him:

Nature is Brahman. There is nothing other than Brahman called Nature. Nature's beauty is, therefore, the beauty of Brahman.

He really sees who sees Brahman in universal nature, whether polluted or pure.

So can nature be used to realise God? Swami Tapovan-ji Maharaj thinks so and says that

If Nature is a great mirror reflecting the power, and beauty and greatness of Brahman, there cannot be any doubt that Nature in all it's nobility will be a help in the realization of His Being.

What is this beauty of nature? It is the same as the Divine Beauty. Apart from Brahman nature has no beauty.

And it is not just in nature that God exist but Swami Tapovan-ji Maharaj says that the God exists everywhere.

What is creation? It is but the manifestation of God in some particular form. As nothing is independent of the God, as there is no existence apart from Him, what is called world is nothing other than God. Nothing can be created without imagination. The extent and scope of His imagination is simply marvellous.

God's power enters everywhere, whether into the hearts of cities or of unexplored mountains.

There is a story from Hindu scriptures that also reiterates the idea that everywhere we see is God or Brahman.

There was this boy call Satyakâma who went to a forest school. In the olden days the teachers used to teach each student according to their ability, aptitude and inclination. Since this boy had never been to a school before or had any form of pre-learning, the teacher knew that he learns more from nature, and thus decided to start from informal learning before using formal methods.

His teacher entrusted him to look after four hundred cows and some bulls and take them to graze. He then asked Satyakâma to come back only after they are one thousand. The teacher then showed him basic worship and rituals that he was supposed to do daily.

Time passed and one day Satyakâma heard a big bull in the herd saying to him, "We are a thousand now; take us back to your teacher. Since, you have looked after us with care and dedication, I will teach you a little about Brahman." .

Satyakâma replied "Sure sir". Then the bull said, "The North is part of the Lord, so is the South. East is part of Lord and so is the West. All the four cardinal points are the four parts of Brahman".

The next day, Satyakâma started back to the school. In the evening he lit the fire and did his prayers and rituals as were taught to him by his teacher. He sat next to the fire when he heard a voice coming from it, "O Satyakâma. You have done your duties daily as were taught by your teacher. I am happy with you and will now teach you a little about Brahman".

Satyakâma replied "Sure sir". Then the fire said, "The Earth is a part of that Lord. The Sky and the Ocean are parts of that Lord. So are Heaven and the Hell. Hence, Earth, Sky, Ocean, Heaven and Hell are all parts of Brahman".

The next day, Satyakâma continue his journey back to the forest school. In the evening, after doing his prayers and rituals, he started his worship at the fire and a swan came to him and said, "I will teach you something about Brahman".

Satyakâma replied "Sure madam". Then the swan said, "This fire which you worship is a part of that Lord. So, are the sun, the moon and the lightning. The fire, sun, moon and lightning, all are parts of that Brahman".

The next day, Satyakâma continue his journey back to the forest school. On the way a bird called Madgu came and said, "I will tell you something about Brahman."

Satyakâma replied "Sure madam". Then the bird said, " Breath is a part of that Lord. And so are the sight, hearing and the mind, all are parts of the Lord. Hence, the sights you see, hearing you do, breath you take and the mind, all are parts of Brahman".

The next day Satyakâma arrived at his forest school and presented himself before his teacher. After paying due respect and reverence to his teacher, he sat down in front of him.

As soon as the teacher saw Satyakâma, he said that "Your face shines like someone who is a knower of Brahman. Who taught you the highest learning". Satyakâma replied "All I have learnt is from the nature. But please, do give me formal teaching as well; since it is said that when one learns from a teacher or Guru, then the teachings are not lost".

The teacher then replied and said, "You have been taught about Brahman by gods themselves. But, since you have requested me to teach you formally as well, I will teach you about Brahman". Then the teacher taught him the same knowledge which he had received from the nature.

In the above story, the bull, the birds and the fire said that everything is part of, or are that one God or Brahman. Hence, Satyakâma learnt that God or Brahman exists everywhere, in all of creation, which is also what Swami Tapovan-ji Maharaj have said.

But what does an ordinary person who cannot yet see God everywhere do? Swami Tapovan-ji Maharaj says that

Why should we try to realise God? Swami Tapovan-
ji Maharaj gives several reasons such as God is The

pleasure that everyone is trying to find in materialistic things; He is eternal; makes everything in the world exist, etc.

People are engaged in the relentless pursuit of ephemeral and limited worldly pleasures. To get at those flimsy joys and to preserve them they waste the precious human life. They appear inordinately proud of such possessions. All these pleasures are but the infinitesimal part of the bliss of Brahman.

A thing appears in one form today, in another form tomorrow and in yet another form the day after. But within all these changing things, there is something, eternal. That is God.

Without a thread there is no garland of flowers, similarly, without God there is no universe. How many billions of worlds are joined to It and exist of It? Who can count or calculate? That It is the source, as Soul or Brahman.

It is at His will that clouds come down as rains, rivers flow, vegetables grow, man enjoys or suffers.

Some mahā-vākyas or "Great Sayings" on the concept of Brahman by Swami Tapovan-ji Maharaj:

Brahman is the ultimate Truth.

God is everywhere and at all times, He sees everything.

Pain as well as pleasure is Brahman and therefore the same. All this world of joy and sorrow is superimposed upon Brahman.

He who has realized God, finds Him everywhere and in everything.

Nothing is, except Brahman.

Brahman appears under different names and in different forms and nothing else.

I will end this chapter with following two wisdom words from Swami Tapovan-ji Maharaj:

All I see is God. The Himalayas are God. The entire earth is God. Everything exists in Him. Everything shines because of His brightness. All beauty is His.

[For one who always sees Brahman] for him Samadhi is of no use, for he has become the embodiment of Samadhi !

3 FAITH

In Śrīmad Bhagavad Gita Lord Shri Krishna has said:

śhraddhāvānllabhate jñānaṁ tat-paraḥ sanyatendriyaḥ

jñānaṁ labdhvā parāṁ śhāntim achireṇādhigachchhati

|| 4.39 ||

Person who has complete faith and works hard at gaining sense and mind control through constant practice can also get to transcendental knowledge. With that transcendental knowledge, one can get eternal peace.

A person with complete faith has total control of his senses and mind as without them, senses and mind would go outwards and faith of such person would waver. Here, Lord Shri Krishna gives another way to obtain the transcendental knowledge that helps in realising God.

Swami Tapovan-ji Maharaj also gave importance to having faith for a spiritual person. According to Him:

Without faith it is impossible for man to reach his spiritual goal.

In spiritual matters (all great religions and all great teachers of the religion agree on this point) it is faith that matters, not intelligence.

With mere intelligence no man has ever attained the highest spiritual experience.

Swami Tapovan-ji Maharaj believed that:

Sraddha (faith) is a wonderful thing indeed. It turns water into theertha, stone into God. All religions of the world are founded on faith. It leads the world forward as a marshal leads his men.

Faith works wonders. It transforms the weak into the strong, the skilled into the skilful, and cowards into heroes.

For people who repose implicit faith in God and His mercy, can there be anything like want? Even in the solitary Himalayan recesses where one hardly ever hears of food, they experience plenty.

When the fire of faith burns within, one cannot feel even the benumbing cold.

And what hinders a person on getting that faith? According to Swami Tapovan-ji Maharaj it is

Sin impedes faith.

It is his sinfulness that drags him down, by tightening the hold of gold and worldly pleasures on his heart and by wheedling him away from other-worldly thoughts and spiritual practices.

And how do we get rid of the sin. Lord Shri Krishna has said that one has to control one's senses and mind so it does not go after *'gold and worldly pleasures'* that takes a person away from spirituality.

4 DESIRES

Hindu scriptures identify six main impediments on the path of spirituality. These are Kama (desire), krodha (anger), lobha (greed), Mada (arrogance), moha (infatuation) and matsarya (jealousy).

Lord Krishna has said in Śrīmad Bhagavad Gita -

dhyāyato vishayān pumsaḥ sangas teshūpajāyate

sangāt sañjāyate kāmaḥ kāmāt krodho 'bhijāyate

||2.62||

Thinking and associating with materialistic things in this world give rise to attachments. These attachments in turn give rise to desires and desires further give rise to anger when they are either not fulfilled or have not given the expected results or happiness and satisfaction that one had initially expected.

Hence, attachment gives rise to desire which is identified as one of the six main impediments on the path of spirituality.

Swami Tapovan-ji Maharaj believed that

Conquest of desire is Kaivalya - the highest goal of man.

Conquest of desire alone leads to fearless, free and happy life.

[Conquest of desire] alone yields absolute peace and supreme
Bliss.

As desire is an outcome of the attachment, the next question that arises is how is it that one gets attachment. Swami Tapovan-ji Maharaj thinks desire is something innate in everyone. Desires are beyond the five senses that we usually use to perceive and understand the world i.e. what we see, hear, touch, taste and smell through we get attached to the worldly things.

Desire is something subtle and beyond the comprehension of the
senses. Our surmises based on externals are therefore liable to
go wrong, and they do often go wrong.

Swami Tapovan-ji Maharaj further says that it is not easy to overcome desire and compares it a multi-headed monster. He says that:

Desire is a Hydra headed monster. Cut off one head and you find several taking its place. Overcome sexual desire and it is soon replaced by the desire of wealth. Overcome that too, then the attachment to the body shows itself with unprecedented strength. Get over that attachment also then the desire for immortal fame calls aloud like a lioness from the caverns of the heart. Even the wisest and the most learned of mankind are ensnared by desire for fame.

Desire for fame is the last infirmity of noble minds. It can be overcome by only wise and heroic minds.

Swami Tapovan-ji Maharaj recommends that only way to overcome desire is to realise Self or God within Self.

Until a man fully realizes Self his mind cannot be completely freed from desire.

He who seeks to conquer desire except through the realization of Self is verily attempting the impossible.

So, overcoming all desires is not an easy feat to do. It requires a lot of patience, perseverance, hard-work and following the teachings and foot-steps of the saints and the sages who have attained God-realisation.

I would end with wisdom word of Swami Tapovan-ji Maharaj:

Until man realizes God, he is a puppet of desires and therefore poor and sorrowful.

5 *MAYA (ILLUSION)*

Swami Tapovan-ji Maharaj says Maya is very powerful and takes control of learned and non-learned equally.

..aiming at pleasure and eagerly longing for the prolongation of life, man goes on revolving with the endless circle of samsara. In our world of opposites, who can separate joy from sorrow, life from death, good repute from ill-repute and cold from heat? Wonderful are the workings of Maya !

The seductive power of the sense objects is an momentary as the flashes of lighting.

There is a story of Lord Shri Krishna and sage Narada in the Hindu scriptures that relates to the power of Maya .

Sage Narada is the son of Lord Brahma and one of the biggest devotee of Lord Vishnu. He has the power to go anywhere in heaven, earth and hell in a flash of milliseconds. He uses his powers to spread devotion and help devotees of Lord Vishnu.

Once sage Narada asked Lord Shri Krishna to give him taste of Maya as he does not understand how come Maya can control hearts and minds of living beings especially of those who have reached certain spiritual level. He was referring to rishi Vishvamitra who after being so austere and having practised and doing penance for centuries and having power to change things and conditions just with his words and intentions digressed from path of spirituality due to power of Maya.

Lord Shri Krishna smiled and said, 'Ok I will one day but let us first go for a short walk'.

They both walked for sometime through forest and then barren lands. Sage Narada enquired. 'Lord. where are we going. I cannot see anything other than desert and a few dead trees'.

Lord Shri Krishna replied, 'Ah, I did not realise! We must have wandered off. Let us go back, but can you please get me some water first as I am too thirsty to walk any more'.

So sage Narada went to seek for water. While looking for water, he saw that there are some girls filling water from a well. Sage Narada was thirsty himself, so he thought why don't I have water myself first and then take some for Lord Shri Krishna.

Sage Narada approached the girls and asked for water to drink. As he was drinking water offered by one of the beautiful girls, he had a strong desire to spend rest of his life with the girl.

He enquired about the family of the girl and offered his hand in marriage. The father of the girl was happy that his daughter would be getting married to such a high-level sage.

So soon sage Narada was married to the girl. Now the girl was no other than the daughter of the chieftain of the clan. So after the marriage, sage Narada was made the king in waiting and after the death of the chieftain, he became, the king of the clan.

Meanwhile, a few years had passed and sage Narada was a well-reputed king with flourishing kingdom, a beautiful queen and father of a few kids.

One day, the neighbouring king attacked sage Narda's kingdom. Sage Narada did not know how to fight -- well really he was a sage he was not a fighter. So he lost the war and the neighbouring king took control of a lot of area of sage Narada's kingdom.

It is said that when problems come they do not come alone; they come in multiples. Sage Narada's kingdom had the worst flood in the history of the wh ole country at the same time. The flooded river broke it's bank and the flow of water was so strong that it swallowed nearly everyone in the kingdom including sage Narada's wife and kids.

Heart-broken and without his position or family, sage Narada just started to walk. He crossed the boundaries of his kingdom into the vast desert. After a long walk, tired and thirsty, sage Narada saw someone sitting alone. Thinking that the person may have some water for him to quench his thirst, he ran to the person saying 'water.. my friend .. can I get some water..'.

Suddenly he heard a familiar voice -- 'Yes, I am still waiting for my water for past 1 hour, Narada, did you get some'. It was Lord Shri Krishna. Sage Narada in shock said, 'Lord, it is so good to see you. Do you know what happened in my life -- I got married, had kids, then the neighbouring king attached and we had the worst floods of the century and I lost my whole family in it.'

Then suddenly as if waking-up, sage Narada said, 'what do you mean 1 hour, how can that be? My whole life passed by in just 1 hour ?'

Lord Shri Krishna smiled and said, 'You wanted to get a taste of my Maya ? It can delude ignorant and learned alike; like you sage Narada, one of the most learned sage and one who is always thinking of Me can get under My Maya and step away from the right path.

Similarly, rishi Vishvamitra who after being so austere and having practised and doing penance for centuries and having power to change things and conditions just with his words and intentions digressed from path of spirituality due to power of Maya'.

Lord Shri Krishna in Śrīmad Bhagavad Gita says that until one has completely surrendered to Him, it is very hard and difficult to overcome His Maya.

daivī hyeṣhā guṇa-mayī mama māyā duratyayā
mām eva ye prapadyante māyām etāṁ taranti te
|| 7.14 ||

Swami Tapovan-ji Maharaj also agrees that it is

very hard to overcome Maya even when one has reached certain spiritual level. He says that:

> *There may be a few great souls who enjoy the state of Samadhi but even their minds and senses are not beyond the reach of the mighty Illusion.*

> *Irresistible indeed is the power of Maya which misleads even the great souls who desire to take the path of wisdom !*

Swami Tapovan-ji Maharaj says that:

> *So long as man, however learned, remains in this bondage of illusion, there is hardly any difference between him and the meanest worm.*

And why did Swami Tapovan-ji Maharaj think that man under illusion is no different to any other creature ? Swami Tapovan-ji Maharaj says that it is because,

> *God has given them both [man and animal] power to know and power to do. Both remain to bodily senses, both seek worldly pleasures and suffer greatly.*

*Man can hardly consider himself superior to other creatures
so long as he fails to use his Reason properly for breaking the
bondage he is in....The sastras esteem them [power to know and
power to do] as the result of great good deeds. With Reason
man has great things to achieve. Properly utilised, it is the chief
requisite for breaking the illusory bondage and realizing God.
But the mere possession of it cannot make man worthier than
other creatures.*

But does that mean all is lost and there is no way
out ? Swami Tapovan-ji Maharaj thinks that there is a
way out. One must realise that they are under Maya,
illusion or bondage and they can take first step in
getting out of Maya with God's grace.

*Only a few virtuous souls with real wisdom realise that
sensuous pleasures which cause bondage are ultimately the
source of sorrow, and cultivate a spirit of detachment in an effort
to attain the Divine Joy.*

*The very awareness of bondage is the result of keen
discrimination.*

And what are the qualities required by someone who wants to get out of Maya. Swami Tapovan-ji Maharaj thinks it is perseverance, faith, true knowledge and detachment.

One may ascend to the highest peak of the Himalayas; but unless one is exceptionally fortunate and possesses tireless industry, deep faith, true knowledge and the highest degree of detachment, one cannot overcome Illusion completely and reach that final blissful state of merger with the Supreme.

6 VAIRAGYA
(INDIFFERENCE TO
WORLDLY THINGS)

Swami Tapovan-ji Maharaj defines Vairagya as indifference to worldly things. On path of God realisation, Swami Tapovan-ji Maharaj identifies Vairagya as an important quality to have. He says that:

Great indeed is the power of Vairagya (indifference to worldly things).

[Vairagya] makes the impossible easily possible.

In Śrīmad Bhagavad Gita Lord Shri Krishna has said:

asanśhayaṁ mahā-bāho mano durnigrahaṁ chalam
abhyāsena tu kaunteya vairāgyeṇa cha gṛihyate
||6.35||

Lord Shri Krishna had been telling Arjuna that he should control his mind and without vacillating do what is right in all situations; to do his right duty, which at that stage was to fight against the injustice that had been done to him and his family. While telling Arjuna all this, Lord Shri Krishna had also been imparting him knowledge about different ways of living rightfully in this world using either analytical knowledge or way of action, or way of renunciation, or way of meditation and so on.

Arjuna replied that whatever Lord Shri Krishna had been telling him makes all sense but mind is very hard to control. It goes from one thought to another; from what seems right at one moment to something else that seems right the other moment; from one want to another and so on.

In replying to Arjuna's comment that it is very hard to restrain or get one's mind under control, Lord Shri Krishna agrees with Arjuna that indeed it is hard. But then He says that control or restrain of mind is crucial as because of uncontrolled or unrestrained mind, one would lose one's goal in life as well as not do one's rightful duty and go from from one birth to another. Then He says that the mind can be brought under control or be restrained by vairagya and constant practice.

There is a saying that '*practice makes a man perfect*'. This is applicable to both materialistic as well as spiritual world. Take for an example of an instrument player such as cellist, pianist, violist; only after years of regular practice does one becomes good enough to play in a concert. Similarly, with years of regularly doing spiritual practices one's mind becomes purified enough to be able to see God in one's lifetime.

Regular practice requires a lot of patience and perseverance. As Thomas Alwa Edison, inventor of light bulb said that '*a genius is 1% inspiration and 99% perspiration*'; similarly mastery over something such as playing an instrument or achieving one's goal requires right direction and more of patience and perseverance.

This becomes much harder for spiritual practices where one's mind gets either bored after sometime or runs towards worldly things and objects. This is where vairagya comes in picture.

Swami Tapovan-ji Maharaj says that:

..true Vairagya is difficult to attain, because desire and attachment springs from multifarious sources.

True Vairagya is the result of thought. The other kinds of Vairagya, resulting from various other causes, can, at best, be only weak, temporary and halting.

Vairagya, as Swami Tapovan-ji Maharaj says, is indifference to worldly things. If indifference to worldly things is not there it is because one still has desires or attachments to the world whether it is towards people, relationships, material gains, comforts and other things or situations that one thinks would give him or her happiness and / or contentment in the world.

When desires and attachment are still there, then the mind keeps getting back to the object of desires or attachment instead of remaining focussed in the spiritual practice.

Let us take an example of a person who moves to a secluded place to continue spiritual practices with less distractions. But, if the person still has desires and attachments, then such person's mind would try to compare the new place with the previous one and come up with reasons of why one should go back or one may get attached to the new place or environment. The person would spend more time on thinking why did he not come here before or just spend most time in looking and appreciating at the new environment and place instead doing his spiritual practice.

That's why Swami Tapovan-ji Maharaj says that these kind of ways of developing vairagya are not permanent. True vairagya comes only when thoughts are in control and they do not go towards things that one desires or can get attached to.

And what happens when one achieves true Vairagya ?
Swami Tapovan-ji Maharaj says that:

*When Vairagya dawns, tenderness changes into hardness,
weakness into strength and grief into joy.*

7 SANYASINS
(RENUNCIATES)

As per Hindu philosophy of life, humans are averaged to live a life of 100 years. With this assumption, life is divided into four periods of approximately 25 years of age. Each of this period is called an ashram. The four ashrams are :

* Brahmacharya or life of student: In this ashram, an individual is supposed to study and learn the basic skills of life and understand how one is supposed to live in this world.

* Gṛhastha or householder: In this ashram, an individual steps into society, use his or her skills that one has gained as a Brahmacharya. They start contributing to society by helping society, earning money, getting married and supporting one's family and society as a whole.

* Vanaprastha or dweller of forest: In this ashram, an individual prepares for the last stage of life that is Sanyasa. He or she starts spending more and more time on contemplation of God and starts handing the skills one has learned and assets one has accumulated over the lifetime to next generation in one's family and society.

* Sanyasa or renunciation: In this ashram, an individual spends most of time on contemplation of God and shares his or her knowledge with people

who want to know and walk on path of God realisation once he or she has realised God.

Swami Tapovan-ji Maharaj used to hold Sanyasa and a true Sanyasin in high regard. He believed that

..a man's samskara-the sum-total of his inborn tendencies inherited from previous lives-turns him into a worldling or a sanyasin.

Hence, one cannot train or practice to be a sanyasin until and unless one has the inert seeds to become one. So what does one need to have to become a sanyasin. Swami Tapovan-ji Maharaj identified that a sanyasin has following traits:

thought of the world to come, straight forwardness and non-violence for the foundations of a sanyasin's life.

Or in other words, a sanyasin does not live for just himself but he is for the world; he cares, works and thinks for the whole world. A sanyasin is straight-forward in his ways and speech. He says as the things are and does not sugar-coat it or hide the truths with words. A sanyasin is non-violent in speech, action or thoughts towards all-beings and creations of the world.

Swami Tapovan-ji Maharaj believed that a true

..sanyasin experiences only bliss, at all places and at all times.

A true sanyasin always felt bliss as he only sees God everywhere in all situations whether he is going through hardship or in comfort; whether he feels sorrow or happiness. For a true sanyasin, body maybe effected by disease or pain but it still does not effect the inner peace or calmness and one sees God's play in all situations.

There is a beautiful story by Ramakrishna Paramahamsa:

A yogi (renunciate) used to live in Dakshineshwar

48

temple where Ramakrishna Paramahamsa used to live. He would hardly come outside the building and spend most of his time in meditation and contemplation of God.

Once there was a big thunder-storm with lot's of lighting and thunder. While everybody ran inside, this yogi came outside the building and started to dance.

When Ramakrishna Paramahamsa asked him why he is outside as he hardly comes outside especially when everyone is running inside to take cover?

The yogi laughed and said that why should he be inside or run away from here? He has come outside to view this beautiful show of the Creator.

The yogi saw God in all things and in all places.

And what is the pre-requisite to becoming a sanyasin? Swami Tapovan-ji Maharaj says that one of the prerequisites to becoming a Sanyasin is to have control over mind and worldly desires.

It hardly requires to be stressed here that the acceptance of sanyasa before one has conquered his desires and acquired perfect control over mind and body, is sinful and will easily prove a passport to hell.

Merely by putting on the saffron robe one cannot shed his desires and inborn tendencies. Passions like lust and greed, lurking in the heart of man, are stirred up in the presence of congenial objects. To nip such passions in the bud requires years of patient effort.

Lord Shri Krishna has expressed similar views in Śrīmad Bhagavad Gita :

yaṁ sannyāsam iti prāhur yogaṁ taṁ viddhi pāṇḍava
na hyasannyasta-saṅkalpo yogī bhavati kaśhchana
|| 6.2 ||

Sanyās is also a Yog. One cannot be called a yogi (or a sanyasin) without renouncing worldly desires.

That's why in most ashrams that follow a monastic lifestyle or sanaysin traditions before one becomes a monk or sanyasin, one has to practice as a brahmachari for a few years where they live and prepare for a life of a sanyasin. Only, once a brahmachari has reached a certain level of expectation, they are given robes of a sanyasin.

Even after being a sanyasin one has to keep a check on oneself to ensure that they are not straying from the path of sanyas and spirituality. As Siddhi mata ji (incarnation of Universal Mother, Neem Karoli Baba, Kainchi dham, Uttrakhand, India) has said that 'Life is like walking on the edge of a sword. You have to watch every step'. This applies especially to one who wants to progress in spiritual life; irrespective of whether one has reached a certain spiritual level or not.

Lord Shri Krishna in Śrīmad Bhagavad Gita says:

śhreyān swa-dharmo viguṇaḥ para-dharmāt sv-anuṣhṭhitāt
svabhāva-niyataṁ karma kurvan nāpnoti kilbiṣham
|| 18.47 ||

By doing one's innate dharma or living as per right conduct and performing the right duties, a person may incur less issues in this life and next lifetime.

As per dharma of a sanyasin is to contemplate on God and live on alms. If he goes out and earns money for living then he is not following his dharma. If a sanyasin has not fully gained control over his or her desires, one would not fully concentrate and spend time on contemplation of God, and hence would not be following his or her own dharma and that's why I believe Swami Tapovan-ji Maharaj said that if someone takes sanyās or renunciation before having control over desires may 'easily prove a passport to hell'.

That is why in Hindu philosophy of life, most are recommended to go through all the ashrams of life one by one since one is a pre-cursor for the other and prepares the person to be ready for the next stage of life. Sanyās being the last stage of life where one has already gained some victory or control over one's worldly desires and the person is ready to go fully in contemplation of God.

Another tip from Swami Tapovan-ji Maharaj for a sanaysin is:

...the sanyasins of the present and the future should learn .. lesson from the experience of their predecessors.

A sanyasin needs to have complete surrender to God. Swami Tapovan-ji Maharaj tells of a beautiful story regarding this:

Once a devout eighteen-year old Christian girl left her hearth and home to follow the Lord. When she renounced all earthly possessions, she kept just a penny for her next meal.

Then she heard a Voice from the sky, "Did you give up everything else trusting to this one penny".

At once she replied, "My Lord ! I came out trusting you, not to the penny" and immediately flung away the coin.

Now trusting solely to the care of the Lord, she proceeded on her way.

For the man who relies on wealth, of what avail is God's aid? For the devotee of God, of what use is worldly wealth?

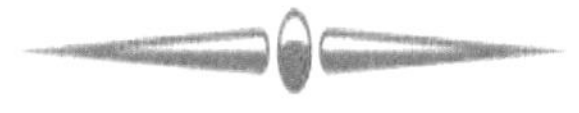

I will end with wisdom words of Swami Tapovan-ji
Maharaj :

[True] Sanyasins are Lord Vishnu in so many shapes.

8 RIVER GANGA

During the discourse between Lord Shri Krishna and Arjuna in the Śrīmad Bhagavad Gita, Arjuna acknowledges that Lord Shri Krishna exists everywhere in the world and pervades all of it. He then requests Lord Shri Krishna to tell about His main manifestations in this world so that he can focus his mind on them. Arjuna knew that for those who cannot see God everywhere, they can start with focusing their minds on His main manifestations. One can realise and see God this way as God and His manifestation are one and the same.

While describing Arjuna about His main manifestations within the world, Lord Shri Krishna says that among the flowing rivers of the world, He is river Ganga.

Lord Shri Krishna in Śrīmad Bhagavad Gita says:

pavanah pavatam asmi ramah shastra-bhritam aham
jhashanam makarash chasmi srotasam asmi jahnavi
||10.31||

Amongst those that purify, I am wind, among the weapon wielders, I am Lord Rama, among the water creatures, I am crocodile and among the flowing rivers, I am the river Ganga.

River Ganga holds an important place since the Vedic times. It along with Her tributaries have been feeding and sustaining the mankind since ages. If one looks into the Indian history, early Indian civilisation came around river Ganga. In fact, some of the main Indian towns are still situated on the banks of River Ganga. Many sages and saints made their homes and performed austerities at Her banks or Her various tributaries.

Swami Tapovan-ji Maharaj recognises the importance of the river Ganga and lovingly calls Her, Mother.

He says:

O Mother Ganga, I am your worshipper and not your critic. I respect you as my supreme goddess, I love and worship you as my mother.

For Indians, especially Hindus', river Ganga plays one or the other role in their lives from birth to death. Giving or putting even a drop of water into a Hindu's mouth at the time of death is an important ritual that is said to liberate the person from the sins that one may have incurred in one's lifetime.

Reiterating river Ganga's importance Swami Tapovan-ji Maharaj says that

The Ganga is not mere water, like lakes or seas. It is Brahma Itself in liquid form. It has incarnated Itself as the holiest water to wash away the sins of the wicked.

Swami Tapovan-ji Maharaj also recognises river Ganga as one of the main manifestation of God and says that:

If purity of mind is essential to the realization of God, devotion to Ganga which is specifically helpful in purifying mind, must be regarded as invaluable to all seekers of Knowledge.

To bathe in the Ganga, to drink the water from Ganga, to worship Mother Ganga, and sing devotional hymns to her - such are the ways of cleansing the heart of all its dross and if such devices fail, it is certain that in these days there exists no other method of heart-purification for man.

While everyone of us cannot be lucky to be living at the shore of river Ganga or have access to Her water, we can still focus our minds on this manifestation of God. That is why Hindus, when taking a bath in the morning sing the following hymn invoking Her presence in the water while taking the bath:

*Gangge Ca Yamune caiva Godaavari Sarasvati Narmade
Sindhu Kaaveri Jale-smin Samnnidhim Kuru ||*

 O Holy Rivers Ganga, Yamuna, Godavari, Saraswati, Narmada, Sindhu and Kaveri; Please make this water holy by your presence.

Let us focus our minds on the river Mother Ganga, seeing in Her the God Himself.

9 *TIPS FOR SPIRITUAL ASPIRANT*

Collection of tips by Swami Tapovan-ji Maharaj that can help any spiritual aspirant:

1. On why a spiritual aspirant is recommended to go through a formal order for God-realisation:

It is a matter of common experience that a boy who attends school progresses much more quickly than another who tries to study at home. Similarly, a spiritual aspirant makes headway far more easily in the company of men who have realized Truth or are constantly trying to realize it.

Spiritual truth is extremely difficult to comprehend. It is only very rarely we come across people who ardently desire to learn it; it is still more rare to find people who are entitled to teach it. Except from well qualified teachers none can understand it properly.

The company of virtuous people turns the wicked into the good, the sinful into the blessed. It clears off the trammels of bondage and sets slaves free. It makes the sad happy.

2. On places that help spirituality:

It is well-known characteristics of beautiful, solitary forests that they intensify man's feelings, whether it is devotion or physical love. It helps concentration in a state of meditation. That is why sadhus resort to such forests to develop their devotion and practice concentration.

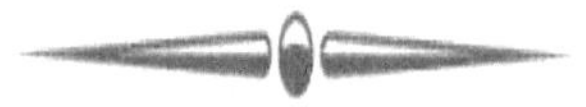

3. On motivating oneself to realise Truth:

Our ancestors were never satisfied until they had fully realized Truth. They did not rest content with hearing spiritual texts quoted from scriptures or expounded by learned teachers.

[Our ancient rishis] never neglected their soul for the enjoyment of worldly pleasures. They firmly believed that the gain of all the world was no compensation for the loss of one's soul. They were never satisfied with anything less than realization.

4. On yoga:

*...the yoga must be of the correct type emanating from the
Upanishads and handed down by the great rishis.*

*Yoga ..consists in attaining complete control over the vacillations
of the restless mind. The process involves eight steps [Yama,
Niyama, Asanas, Pranayama, Pratyahara, Dharana,
Dhyana, Samadhi].*

5. On warnings for a spiritual aspirant:

God shines everywhere, in stone and earth and water, but men who have not overcome their ego fail to find the Resplendent One anywhere.

Conceit of Self in one's intelligence, senses and body is egotism.

"I" leads to "Mine" and for the sinner who is immersed in this "I" and "Mine" the realization of God's Omnipresence is verily impossible.

The truth is, the greatest siddhi is but of the earth, the greatest siddha is yet a worldling. He still remains a slave to passions.

The fewer one's possessions, the greater are one's enjoyment and freedom - it is an incontrovertible truth learnt by experience.

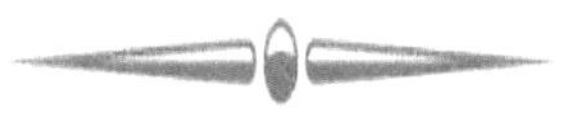

6. On how should one live life in this world:

*There is nothing incompatible between the realization of the soul
and the maintenance of wife and children or cultivation of one's
lands. You may be politician, social reformer or religious leader.
Whatever you be, do your work with the knowledge of the soul.*

*The work of the man who does it with the knowledge of soul,
will certainly be more efficient and more conducive to the welfare
of the world than that of the man who works without that
knowledge.*

7. On when a spiritual aspirant has a slip:

*When a man is undergoing spiritual discipline it may so
happen that he slips down at times. That is, the devotee's mind
and senses may, sometimes, lapse from their high state of purity,
but that should not dishearten him. On the contrary, he must
cling to his ideal and cherish his hope. He who believes that fall
is antecedent to rise will never give way to despair. If you retreat
a few steps to add to the momentum of your forward leap, the
withdrawal should not be regarded as setback.*

8. On waking-up to life purpose:

*life in human form fails of its purpose if it ends without the
supreme realization. Without that realization one cannot have
peace or real happiness.*

*Everyone who is born must dies; yet who remembers the
inevitable end? Daily, people see hundreds of creatures falling
victims to Death. Still they fancy themselves immortal. Smaller
fishes with their young ones play about in the mouth of the
whale; similarly, man with his wife and children, name and
fame, sports with Death.*

9. On Learning:

When a man has realized the eternal Truth by distinguishing between the true and the untrue with the help of concrete objects, he may no longer require that mode of worship, but until such realization, the substitution of the unreal for the Real, is not undesirable or purposeless.

There is no doubt, careful observers can learn not only through scriptures but also through daily experiences, something about the wonderful power of God.

Except those who have detached themselves completely from the world, who possess the talent of wise and careful thought, none can hope to understand Brahma Vidya, even indirectly, that is even intellectually.

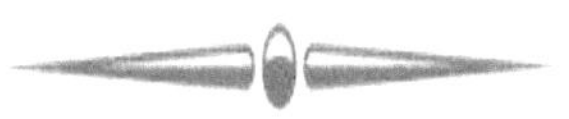

10 *FOR YOUR OWN CONTEMPLATION*

Some of other Words of Wisdom from Swami Tapovan-ji Maharaj for your own contemplation:

God is Truth, Truth is God.

The first duty of those who want to see Truth face to face is the constant hearing of holy texts and contemplation. Such practice depends upon inevitably on solitude and peace of mind.

The Truth of truths is contained in the Vedantic theory that only the One thing which is unlimited and which is the basis of everything else, is the Reality. Modern Science supports this theory with its deduction that all universe originates from an unlimited and indestructible force.

Whether others accept it or not, Truth is always Truth. That Truth is One can never be denied.

Love and devotion (Bhakti) are not two different things.

Love for those above us, is called Bhakti - love for the gods or God is of this type. Love for one's equal is called friendship.

When stainless devotion to God gets deep-rooted in the mind of man, we consider the object of his existence already attained.

Bhakti and service are inextricably connected. When there is bhakti there will, certainly, be the willingness to serve. They who worship God with love, love everything in the form of God.

Devotion, even if it is the outcome of traditional faith and not the result of thought and reasoning, is still laudable, because the object of our devotion is the Controller of everything and Giver of everything and without His help we cannot even eat or sleep.

Miraculous indeed is love. Its sweetness and power are alike great.

There is no limit to God's mercy.

God's mercy alone is worth the name. It is an ocean of absolute kindness.

Why should faithful grieve? In any state, under any conditions, the faithful have cause to rejoice.

According to ancient aphorisms, God's mercy is at the root of all good fortune; man's effort is only secondary.

What is there to shield us from perils except our own discretion and God's mercy?

11 ADDENDUM

LORD KRISHNA

Lord Krishna is the eighth avatar of Lord Vishnu, one of the trinity God in Hinduism. He is the God of protection, compassion, tenderness and love. The name "Krishna" originates from the Sanskrit word Kṛṣṇa, which is primarily an adjective meaning "black", "dark", "dark blue" or "the all attractive". Lord Krishna is also one of the main characters in Mahābhārata and is central to many of the main stories of the epic.

The Mahābhārata is one of the two major Sanskrit epics of ancient India, the other being the Rāmāyaṇa. It narrates the struggle between two groups of cousins in the Kurukshetra War and the fates of the

Kaurava and the Pāṇḍava princes and their successors. Śrīmad Bhagavad Gita is one of the principal works and stories in the Mahābhārata.

- From Wikipedia

ŚRĪMAD BHAGAVAD GITA

Śrīmad Bhagavad Gita or simply 'Gita' or 'The Song by God' is part of Mahābhārata, one of the main epics of Hindu scriptures. It is said to be written by Lord Ganesha and narrated by Sage Veda Vyasa. Gita consists of 700-verses where Lord Krishna guides the Pandava prince Arjuna when he was in dilemma of whether he should go ahead with the war against his own cousins, close relatives and teachers or leave the war to become a monk. Lord Shri Krishna outlines how a person when faced with dilemmas of life, live in this world while doing his duties as well as pursue the spiritual path with the aim of attaining liberation or release from cycles of birth and rebirth.

Gita presents a synthesis of Hindu ideas about dharmtheistic bhakti, and the yogic ideals of moksha. The text covers Jñāna, Bhakti, Karma and Rāja yogas, incorporating ideas from the Samkhya-Yoga philosophy. The Gita's call for selfless action inspired many leaders of the Indian independence movement including Bal Gangadhar Tilak and Mahatma Gandhi, the latter referring to it as his "spiritual dictionary".

Śrīmad Bhagavad Gita is one of the main influencer for many of the Hindu religious systems such as: - Sri Ramanuja Viśiṣṭ ādvaita or non-dualistic system, - Sri Madhvacharya's Dvaita or dualist school of thought, - Sri Vallabha Acharya advaita or pure monism school of thought to name a few.

The other main scriptures depicting Lord Shri Krishna are the Harivamsa, the Bhagavata Purana, and the Vishnu Purana.

- From Wikipedia

SAGE NARADA

Śage Narada or Narada Muni, is a sage divinity, famous in Hindu traditions as a travelling musician and storyteller, who carries news and enlightening wisdom. He is one of mind-created children of Lord Brahma, the creator god. He appears in a number of Hindu texts, notably the Mahābhārata, regaling Yudhishthira with the story of Prahalada and the Rāmāyana as well as tales in the Puranas. In Indian texts, Narada travels to distant worlds and realms (Sanskrit: lokas).

He is depicted carrying a khartal (musical instrument) and the veena, and is generally regarded as one of the great masters of the ancient musical instrument which he uses to accompany his singing of hymns, prayers, and mantras.

In the Vaishnavism tradition of Hinduism, he is presented as a sage with devotion to the preserver deity Vishnu. Vaishnavas depict him as a pure, elevated soul who glorifies Vishnu through his devotional songs, singing the names Hari and Narayana, demonstrating bhakti yoga. The Narada Bhakti Sutra is attributed to him.

He would usually make his presence known by vocally chanting "Narayana, Narayana" before appearing in a scene. Other texts named after Sage Narada including the Narada Purana and the Nāradasmŕti (pre 6th century CE text), the latter called the "juridical text par excellence" and representing the only Dharmaśāstra text that deals solely with juridical matters while ignoring those of righteous conduct and penance.

- From Wikipedia

ARJUNA

Shri Krishna tells Śrīmad Bhagavad Gita to Arjuna

Arjuna also known as Partha and Dhananjaya, is one of the major characters of the Indian epic Mahābhārata. In the epic, he is the third among Pandavas, the five sons of Pandu. The family formed part of the royal line of the Kuru Kingdom.

In the Mahābhārata war, Arjuna was a key warrior from the Pandava side and slew many warriors including Karna. Before the beginning of the war, his mentor, Lord Shri Krishna gave him the supreme knowledge of Śrīmad Bhagavad Gita to overcome his moral dilemmas.

- From Wikipedia

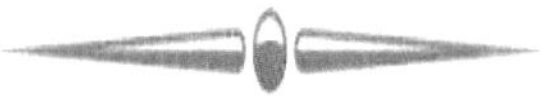

NEEM KAROLI BABA

Neem Karoli Baba or Neeb Karori Baba or lovingly called as Maharaj-ji by his followers is also known as incarnation of Lord Hanuman. He is said to be born as Lakshman Narayan Sharma in the village Akbarpur near Farrukhabad in Uttar Pradesh, India.

During His wandering days He was known by various names such as Lakshman Das Baba, Handi Wallah Baba, Tikonia Walla Baba and Talliaya Baba to name a few.

Maharaj-ji did not differentiate anyone based on their caste, creed, colour, sex or status. The only thing He would look at is the heart, bhavas or emotional frame of the person who is meeting Him. He would give unconditional love without judging one's past karmas and background. He has the ability to change one's heart with love and to make it more receptive to see positive side of humanity and bring out what's best in a person.

- From the book Maa-Maharaj-ji's Grace; Blessings of Siddhi Maa and Neem Karoli Baba

SIDDHI MA

Siddhi Ma also known as silent saint, is an incarnation of the Universal Mother; who is Mother to all beings, big or small, rich or poor, and exists in every speck and corner of this universe. Like a mother protects her child, Maa protects us all from being getting lost in the deep depths of this world. She is the true Mother who showers selfless love upon all of us and has genuine concern for everyone's well-being irrespective whether they are humans, animals, birds, insects, plants or nature.

As a mother, She has not only fulfilled people's wishes but also provided nourishment to their souls. Her heart of gold has been experienced by everyone who has met Her. Her kindness, compassion, thoughtfulness and humbleness are beyond comparison. Her divine aura is so blissful and has a magical power to bless, heal and comfort all who come in contact with Her.

- From the book Maa-Maharaj-ji's Grace; Blessings
                of Siddhi Maa and Neem Karoli Baba

RAMAKRISHNA PARAMAHAMSA

Ramakrishna Paramahamsa was considered as an incarnation of God, an Indian Hindu mystic, and religious leader who lived in Bengal in 19th-century. Ramakrishna Paramahamsa approached his religious life through the path of devotion to the Goddess Kali (incarnation of Supreme Mother), and by observance of various elements from Tantra, Vaishnav Bhakti, and Advaita Vedanta, as well as experiences with Christianity and Islam.

At one time, He practised various religions, realised and proclaimed that all paths of religion leads onto the same God, the same energy.

According to Ramakrishna Paramahansa,

Wherever I look, I see men quarrelling in the name of religion - Hindus, Mohammedans, Brahmos, Vaishnavas, and the rest. But they never reflect that He who is called Krishna is also called Siva, and bears the name of the Primal Energy, Jesus, and Allah as well - the same Rama with a thousand names. A lake has several Ghats. At one, the Hindus take water in pitchers and call it ' Jal ' ; at another the Mussalmans take water in leather bags and call it ' pani '. At a third the Christians call it ' water '. Can we imagine that it is not ' Jal ', but only ' pani ' or ' water '? How ridiculous! The substance is One under different names, and everyone is seeking the same substance; only climate, temperament, and name create differences. Let each man follow his own path. If he sincerely and ardently wishes to know God, peace be unto him! He will surely realize Him.

Ramakrishna Paramahansa left His mortal body in August 1886. Some of His disciples started an organisation led by Swami Vivekananda called Ramakrishna mission. Swami Vivekananda was an enlightened being who is credited to have introduced Vedanta and yoga to the western world.

Ramakrishna mission is a 'worldwide, non-political, non-sectarian spiritual organisations which is engaged in various forms of humanitarian, social service activities for more than a century. Monks and lay people would jointly undertake propagation of practical vedanta, and various forms of social service, such as running hospitals, schools, colleges, hostels, rural development centres, etc, and conducting massive relief and rehabilitation work for victims of earthquakes, cyclones and other calamities, in different parts of India and other countries. They conduct the service without any distinction of caste, religion or race as they see the living God in everyone'.

- From Wikipedia, and Ramakrishna Mission, Belur Math, India

SWAMI SIVANANDA SARASWATI

Swami Sivananda or Swami Sivananda Saraswati was a Hindu spiritual teacher, and a proponent of Vedanta. Swami Sivananda was born as Kuppuswami in 1887 Pattamadai, in the Tirunelveli district of Tamil Nadu. He studied medicine and served in British Malaya as a physician for several years before taking up monasticism. He was the founder of the Divine Life Society (DLS) in 1936, Yoga-Vedanta Forest Academy in 1948 and Sivananda Ashram, the headquarters of the DLS in Rishikesh one of towns situated on banks of river Ganges.

Swami Sivananda authored of over 200 books on yoga, Vedanta, and a variety of subjects helping spiritual aspirants in realisation of God. He had many disciples, two of the including Swami Chidananda Saraswati who became the president of DLS after Swami Sivananda passed away in 1963 and Swami Krishnananda Saraswati who took over as general secretary of DLS.

- From Wikipedia

SWAMI TAPOVAN-JI MAHARAJ

Swami Tapovan Maharaj was born in 1889 in Kerala one of the southern states of India. His mother, Kunjamma and father Achuthan Nair named him Chippukkutty.

He showed high inclination towards spirituality from early childhood. He did home schooling and learnt English, Malayalam (the native language of Kerala) and Sanskrit. He also learned poetry, drama, grammar and logic but spent most of His time in doing spiritual practices.

He won appreciation from many renowned poets of His time for His literary works and even edited for a magazine called 'Gopala Krishna'. On requests from His friends, He delivered lectures on religion, Vedanta, and such subjects that were full of deep knowledge but still easy to understand for general public.

After both His parents passed away and his younger brother got settled in life, Swami Tapovan Maharaj left Kerala on the day of Janmasthami, the birthday of Lord Shri Krishna that usually falls in the months of August-September (months vary as per the Hindu lunar calendar) in 1923 to become a renunciate.

He took sanyasa from Swami Janardanagiri-ji. His spirit of dispassion, His spirit of sacrifice, and His thirst for knowledge increased His fame and He had a lot of followers in a short time. People including both men and women started to come and sit at His feet all day long, eager to learn and study Vedanta from Him. Swami Chinmayananda Maharaj who was a disciple of Swami Sivananda Maharaj, a contemporary of Swami Tapovan-ji Maharaj was also sent by His Guru to study Vedanta under His guidance.

He loved the Himalayas and remained there for the rest of His life. He documented some of His Himalayan travels to help spiritual aspirants understand not just the beauty of Himalayas but also It's sacredness and the various pilgrim spots and areas.

These were document in books called '*Wanderings in the Himalayas*' and '*Kailasa Yatra*'.

Swami Tapovan-ji Maharaj left His mortal body in the early hours of 16 January 1957.

- From the book Wanderings in the Himalayas, and Wikipedia

SWAMI CHINMAYANANDA MAHARAJ

Swami Chinmayananda Saraswati was born as Balakrishna Menon on 8 May 1916 in Kerala, the southern state of India.

As a young man he joined journalism and got his first job as a journalist at The National Herald. As a journalist he wanted to write an exposé on the sadhus and went to Swami Sivananda's ashram in Rishikesh to investigate and bring out an article on how the swamis were bluffing the masses.

Swami Sivananda opened Balakrishna's eyes and on 25 February 1949 he decided to become a renunciate, a sanyasi and got the name of Chinmayananda or "bliss of pure Consciousness". Swami Sivananda blessed him to go out to one of the greatest Vedantic masters of his time, Swami Tapovan-ji Maharaj to study and devote the next few years his pursuing study of the Vedanta.

In 1951, with blessings of his guru Swami Sivananda, Chinmayananda decided to bring the teachings of Vedanta to the masses. In 1953, on being pressed by some of his supporters, Swami Chinmayananda formed a worldwide non-profit organisation named Chinmaya Mission which in Sanskrit means "pure Knowledge" or misssion of "pure knowledge". The mission initially worked in small batches to study religion and philosophy in a systematic manner.

On 6 March 1965, Swami Chinmayananda started delivering Vedantic knowledge internationally with initially doing lectures in 18 countries: Thailand, Hong Kong, Japan, Malaysia, United States, Mexico, Spain, United Kingdom, Belgium, the Netherlands, Sweden, Germany, Denmark, France, Switzerland, Italy, Greece and Lebanon.

Meanwhile, in 1964 Swami Chinmayananda and S. S. Apte worked together to form Vishva Hindu Parishad (VHP). Swami Chinmayananda was elected as president and Apte as general secretary of the new organisation. VHP a formed to "awake(n) the Hindus and to make them conscious of their proud place in the comity of nations".

Swami Chinmayananda passed away on 24 December 1991 after working hard to promote Hinduism and Vedantic knowledge for forty plus years all over the world.

The Chinmaya Mission established by Swami Chinmayananda is still going strong with it's mission of spreading spirituality and Vendata knowledge throughout the world. It has projects in the fields of youth and children education, providing medical facilities, rural development, and environment related projects all over India and in many foreign communities such as Australia, England, New Zealand, Nigeria, South Africa, the United States to name a few.

- From Wikipedia

GANGA RIVER

River Ganga is a trans-boundary river of Asia. The river basin covers parts of four countries, India, Nepal, China, and Bangladesh; and within India covering eleven Indian states. The main stem of the Ganges begins at the town of Devprayag, in India at the confluence of the Alaknanda, which is the source stream in hydrology on account of its greater length, and the Bhagirathi, which is considered the source stream in Hindu Mythology.

The 2,525 km (1,569 miles) river rises in the western Himalayas in the Indian state of Uttarakhand. It flows south and east through the Gangetic plain of North India, receiving the right-bank tributary, the

Yamuna, which also rises in the western Indian Himalayas, and several left-bank tributaries from Nepal that account for the bulk of its flow.

The Ganges is a lifeline to millions of people who live in its basin and depend on it for their daily needs. It has been important historically, with many former provincial or imperial capitals on its banks or the banks of tributaries and connected waterways. The river is home to approximately 140 species of fish, 90 species of amphibians, and also reptiles and mammals, including critically endangered species such as the gharial (type of crocodile found in Indian subcontinent) and South Asian river dolphin.

The Ganges is the embodiment of all sacred waters in Hindu mythology. She is considered Mother by Hindus as She feeds and takes care of Her children. Local rivers are said to be like the Ganges and are sometimes called the local Ganges. The Ganges is a sacred river to Hindus along every fragment of its length. The Ganges is invoked whenever water is used in Hindu ritual and is therefore present in all sacred waters.

EPILOGUE

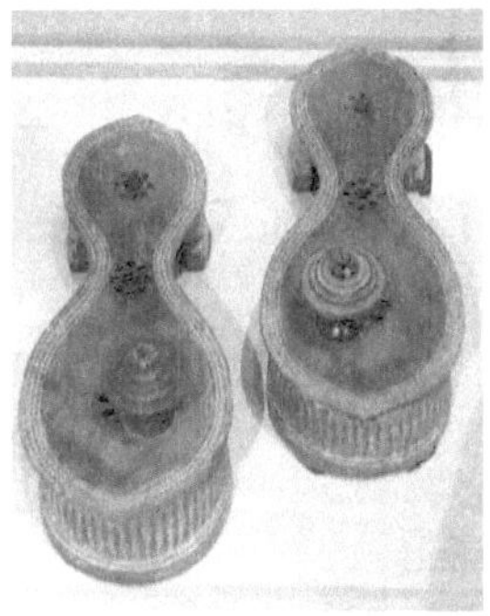

Om Sarvam Shri Gurudev Krishnarpanam Astu

Om Tat Sat

OTHER BOOKS BY THE AUTHOR

1. Neem Karoli Baba, Siddhi Ma & Sayings of Others
- A Śrīmad Bhagavad Gita Perspective,
     Anjaneya Prakash Publications, Feb 2023.

ABOUT THE AUTHOR

Pt. Aswadhnath Anantajit

has a keen interest in the words of wisdom by various saints and Gurus. He believes that Śrīmad Bhagavad Gita is the essence of all the Vedas and Upanishads. One can find all the answers of life, whether spiritual or worldly in Śrīmad Bhagavad Gita, if it is understood correctly. Studying and understanding deeper meaning of the verses in Śrīmad Bhagavad Gita is a lifelong quest - one gets new insights each time one reads them.